NÉSTOR CONTRERAS PINEDA

CHINA: A COLOSSUS WITH CRYSTAL SLIPPERS

Nestor Contreras P. (Caracas, 1947) is a retired military officer and university teacher. Between 1996 and 2005 he was head of the Department of Strategic Studies of the Superior School of the Venezuelan army. He has been Professor at the Institute of High Studies of the National Defense, staff schools of the Venezuelan National Armed Guard, Navy and as well as schools of logistics, artillery, and infantry of the Venezuelan army . He holds a PhD in Education and master´s degrees in Security and Defense, Science and Military Arts and Human Resources Management. He holds diplomas in Public Management, Logistics Management and War Staff. Founder and Director of the magazine Arte y Ciencia Militar.

Other titles of the author: El Sistema de Desarrollo Profesional Avanzado (2004), La Planificación Sistémica (2004), ¿Cómo Generar Pensamiento Estratégico? (2004) and Aprenda Estrategia de la Historia (2004), published by the Carlos Soublette Foundation. Colección Postmodernidad: La Filosofía, la Ciencia y la Técnica en la Formación del Paradigma de la Postmodernidad (versions in French, Italian and Portuguese); Educación en Postmodernidad; Crisis Financiera Mundial: Origen, Evolución y Perspectiva; Globalización: el Modo de Producción de la Postmodernidad, y Aprendizaje Organizacional: un Camino Hacia la Postmodernidad; Ejércitos de la Postmodernidad. USA Army. Colección Estrategia: Entrene su Mente Para la Estrategia; Metodología Sistémica del Aprendizaje Organizacional y Metodología Sistémica de la

Planificación Estratégica. Colección Geopolítica: El Regreso de Rusia al Escenario Político Global (2016). The three collections published by amazon.

English titles: Systemic Methodology of Strategic Planning (2015); Systemic Methodology of the Organizational Learning (2015); Train your Mind for Strategy 2015, Philosophy, Science and Technology in Postmodernity (2015) and The Return of Russia to the Global Political Stage (2016), publishes by Amazon.

INTRODUCTION

The disappearance of the Soviet Union left a void in the international political scene and the United States stood as the only global power. Although the disappearance of the country that generated most of the conflicts during the Cold War provoked the freedom of those nations that had been under communist rule for decades, the predominance of a hegemonic power and the poor decisions of mediocre leadership gave the fret with the global political balance and provoked a greater evil: planetary terrorism. Thus, the hegemony of a single country did not bring positive consequences for the concert of nations, and the world is now plunged into a war without limits or barracks. The emergence of a power that maintains a healthy balance in international relations is therefore a necessity. However, there is no candidate with the potential of becoming the counterweight of the United States. China's economic success created a false illusion; the fact is that it is very far from occupying a relevant place in the world political scene. This book is intended to explain the reasons behind this assertion. In Chapter I, The Insurgency of a Colossus, we present the only country that is in a position to compete with the United States and occupy a place of preponderance in the international political and economic scene: the People's Republic of China.

In Chapter II, Geopolitics of the East, we describe the intricate web of relationships that are present in the East of the planet. The future of world society is decided in that region of the world; there is settled, in vast territories mostly depopulated, the majority of humanity. Ethnic and cultural diversity is so marked that it is inevitable that conflicts will be manifested every moment.

The economic potential of this secluded corner, for Westerners, is immeasurable; that is transformed into wealth and welfare depends on peace being maintained and the United States and China agreeing.

In Chapter III, Marx Versus Smith, we try to summarize the path China has taken to transform its economy. The model is strange. A combination of Marxism and capitalism. In the first decades it seemed that the idea was good, the unusual economic growth made the majority think that the Chinese had reached the perfect recipe: labor almost in conditions of slavery and Western technology. It worked for a while, today the contradictions are emerging with all their force and the model makes waters everywhere. In Chapter IV, A True Colossus, we present to the Hegemon: the United States of America. There is no chance that China will become a world power. Neither in the short, medium or long term. The real recipe is a combination of democracy and capitalism; without it, the Asian giant will remain where it is: playing a secondary role in the international political scene.

I The Insurgency of a Colossus

People's Republic of China

The People's Republic of China is located in East Asia. With a population of one thousand three hundred million inhabitants is the country with the largest population in the world; closely followed by the Republic of India. Although in terms of the Gross Domestic Product (GDP) can be considered as the world's first economy; its contradictions, deficiencies, distortions and limitations make this condition in a precarious balance. The Communist Party has ruled the country since October 1, 1949, when Mao Zedong proclaimed the People's Republic of China. The capital of the country is the city of Beijing and its territorial division includes 22 provinces, 5 autonomous regions, 4 municipalities under central jurisdiction —Beijing, Tianjin, Shanghai and Chongqing— and two special administrative regions - Hong Kong and Macao. In addition, China claims as its own the island of Taiwan, whose current political status is that of an Independent State: The Republic of China, over a surface area of approximately 9.6 million km2,

China has borders with fourteen States. Its surface is vast and diverse and includes steppes, deserts, Gobi and Taklamakán, subtropical forests in the south, mountain ranges, Himalayas, Karakorum, Pamir and Tian Shan, mighty rivers, Yangtze and Amarillo, that run between the Tibetan plateau and the Eastern coasts . Its shores extend over 14,500 km in the Pacific Ocean and include the Yellow, Bohai, East China and South China Seas.

Since its creation, and for millennia, it was ruled by dynasties: hereditary monarchies. The first were the Xia, whose traces are hidden between myths and legends, and the Qin, forging the first Chinese empire. In October 1971, China entered the United Nations and began a political change that transformed China, in only decades, into a world economic power.

The People's Republic of China has an ambiguous form of government that defines itself as communist and socialist. If we add the concepts of authoritarianism and corporatism we could perhaps understand this complexity that allows the ideas of Karl Marx to coexist with those of Adam Smith in a mixture that has facilitated China's transition to capitalism, but, will soon generate a critical mass of contradictions that will surely threaten this unusual political-economic experiment that combines the worst of politics with the infamous market.

China's fundamental problems are: concentration of power in the hands of a minority, widespread corruption, growing inequality, slow growth and environmental pollution. On the whole they could prevent their hopes of becoming a world power from fading. These factors make their political, economic and social balance precarious, and this is always on the verge of disaster. For a few decades, the rapid growth of its economy led to the belief that China would rapidly transform and reach a level of prosperity similar to that of the Western powers in a very short time. The truth is that the more it thrives at the economic level, the more it sinks into its own contradictions.

The worst thing for China is that it has already exhausted the effectiveness of the levers that generated its unusual growth. Western enterprises took little time to respond to the challenge of competition for goods produced by a low-cost production apparatus that was based almost exclusively on the intensive use of a labor force that was working almost in slavery. To compensate for this comparative advantage of the Chinese, the West mutated its productive apparatus and used advanced technology to regain its competitive advantage.

In the coming decades, their thinking machines will lower costs and facilitate the placement of cheap, high-quality products on the world market. Artificial intelligence will be the basis of a new production system that will wipe out the already obsolete Chinese manufacturing model.

While the West already uses deep learning to equip its robots with a human-like cognitive capacity, the Chinese continue to depend on semi-literate workers to support their productive apparatus. Neither have the Chinese achieved the perfect combination of technology giants of the West, Google, Amazon, Apple and Tesla, among others, and their tiny entrepreneurial companies. Despite the effort and capital invested in research and entrepreneurship, the Chinese have not been able to compete with the West in what can be considered the basis of their current success: the free and spontaneous generation of ideas. Under the Communist regime, Chinese society will never reach the maturity it requires to generate prosperity for all its members. Material wealth has not been able to compensate for the absence of freedom. To stay in power, the leadership of the Communist Party needs to keep its repressive apparatus in tune and inhibit free will and individual freedoms. This is not precisely the best breeding ground for the ideas China needs to get out of the quagmire in which it has gotten itself; if the political regime does not change, China will fall back and lose how much it has achieved in the last thirty years: its own contradictions will be responsible for a debacle of such magnitude.

Chinese society

The intention of the political leadership to keep society in harmony faces the social distortion generated by discrimination against minority ethnicities. About 56 racial groups live in the country; the *Han* are the most numerous, with 91% of the total population, about 1.2 billion inhabitants. Although this majority group is by itself the largest in the world, more than 120 million Chinese belong to other ethnic groups; represent approximately

8% of the total population and occupy 64% of the territory of the country. If it were a sovereign state, this would be the eighth of the world. Among the largest ethnic groups are the Mongols, Uyghurs and Kazakhs who occupy the arid regions of the north and northwest; the Tibetans in the western highlands; the Zhuang, located in the autonomous region of Guanxi, bordering Vietnam; in the southwestern provinces (Yunnan, Ghizhou and Sycuan), an extraordinary mosaic of ethnic groups coexist with the Han Chinese. On the east coast of the island of Taiwan, the latter coexist with ten minority groups, most notably the Ami.

These minority groups occupy border areas of great strategic importance because of their location and the abundance of natural resources. In most cases these groups of the Chinese population share historical, cultural, racial and religious ties with the populations of neighboring countries. Discrimination over which they have been subjected for centuries has not allowed them to integrate into Chinese society and, on the contrary, increasingly reinforce the elements of their own cultural identity, and are more likely to solve their problems by Internal conflicts that threaten China's political stability. Mughals, Tibetans and Uyghurs are in open rebellion and against the control of the central government.

The Islamization of Central Asia is a serious problem for China; due to the fluid contact between Chinese and Central Asian Uyghurs. The Uighurs is a mayor Muslim ethnic group living in northwestern China, mainly in the Uyghur Autonomous Region of Siankiang, and in some Central Asian countries: Uzbekistan, Kazakhstan and Kyrgyzstan. Of the 20 million Uighurs, at least 8 million are in favor of the autonomy of China's central control. Jihadist groups in Iraq and Syria have been training dissident factions of the Uyghur people. In recent years, there have been several attacks, attributed to the ethnic group in question, with bombs in the Guanghi region. The alliance between radical Uyghurs and extremist jihadist groups is a very difficult equation to solve. If China does not resolve it peacefully, how it has been doing so, the intensification of the current insurance conflict will threaten its internal stability, not only by the action of the Uyghurs, but also by the intensification of conflicts with the other minority ethnic groups.

The central government has been trying to pacify regions in conflict with projects such as the Silk Road. However, the deceleration of the Chinese economy makes it difficult to materialize this project in the short and medium term, and, on the contrary, in the same period, it could exacerbate the spirits and provoke the intensification of racial tensions and the increase of terrorist attacks.

For their part, Tibetans use intelligence more than force. The powerful influence exerted by its leader, the Dalai Lama, on world society causes more inconvenience to Chinese diplomacy than the Uighur attacks. Every word of this charismatic monk puts China in the sights of world public opinion. Apart from the specific problem of social discrimination affecting minority groups, social inequality affects the whole population. This is one of the most unequal on the planet. The greatest inequality is between those living in the countryside or the city. In the rural area less than 10% of their young people finish high school, while in the cities 70% do. At the age of fifteen, the majority of young peasants left school because of lack of study opportunities.

Although millions of Chinese have emerged from poverty in the last few decades, hundreds of millions are in the same conditions as in the past. The rural population does not have access to well-paid jobs or to health care, adequate housing or a social security scheme. Those who migrate to cities in search of better conditions are treated as second-class citizens who do not have the same rights as local workers. In contrast, in the city millions go to universities and most people in the middle class have their own homes and decent jobs. And as if that were not enough, Chinese society has a demographic imbalance that makes it difficult to replace workers who are of retirement age, as reported in an article in The Economics magazine:

> Decades ago, the Chinese government could have argued that the country was too populated or too poor to accept immigrants. Chinese women now have less than 1.6 children on average, well below the replacement rate, and by 2012 the working-age population declined for the first time. However, China is already succumbing to the problems that many countries face as they become richer and their

workforce better educated. It has a serious shortage of social workers, care staff and nurses, jobs that most Chinese are unwilling to fill. That deficit will grow over the next decade as China's population ages. Most rich countries attract immigrants to perform such functions, but in September the Chinese government reiterated that visas for unskilled or service workers would be strictly limited[1].

How to solve a problem of this importance for the productive apparatus in a country that has a population that already has 1.3 billion inhabitants, and that was caused by the same authorities with their demographic control measures that allowed only one child per couple. Difficulties such as that described have their origin in hasty and authoritarian decisions that ignore the fundamental rights of its population. That is China that intends to replace the United States as the first world power.

II GEOPOLITICS OF THE EAST

Geopolitics of the Asia Pacific region

The Asia-Pacific region is the part of the planet that includes a good portion of East Asia, Southeast Asia and Oceania. It could also include the countries of America that are on the east coast of the Pacific Ocean: Canada, Chile, the United States, Mexico, Peru and Russia. It could also join Australia and the Pacific island nations. In general, it could be said that there is no clear definition, so that it will be the context within which a particular issue is treated as the best reference to establish its conformation and limits.

Each day that passes the global influence of this region increases, as well as say an article by Ash Carter: "The Asia-Pacific area is becoming a world center of gravity in the political and military economic" [1].

In this region two opposing dynamics have begun to converge. On the one hand, the United States tries to maintain the status quo to retain its position as the hegemonic power. On the other hand, China intends to extend its influence beyond its immediate surroundings. Although in the short and medium term it is not clear that the latter can increase its military and naval power to compete, either in the regional or global scenario, with the former, the tension between them could lead to undesired incidents.

Despite the fact that China defends its right to occupy its place in the global scenario and to expand its influence without the interference of the United States, the economic interdependence between both has avoided tensions and the reduction of the risk to a confrontation of war. The accelerated economic growth that China has experienced over the last five years has forced it to increase its presence in the international geopolitical arena. The control of sea routes in the China Sea is key to maintaining the flow of goods that this country requires to sustain a continuously growing productive apparatus. This appetite has generated a series of disputes with both its neighbors in the region and with the Western powers, especially with the United States.

This aquatic space has an importance that surpasses the economic. The United States dominates the global stage, and if China intends to assume the role of superpower it must extend its area of influence. What better scope than the immediate: the sea that surrounds it. The economic success achieved in the last decades has allowed China to expand its area of economic influence: it has tightened ties with countries on all continents and displaced its northern rival in some regions. Now he can use this relationship to expand his geopolitical influence. However, it does not seem like the best time. The financial crisis of 2008 slowed its economic growth and exposed its internal weakness. China had already been taking the first steps towards the conquest of the planet; began with the strengthening of its military power. He has built decades of sophisticated weaponry: advanced submarines, fifth-generation fighter jets, ballistic missiles and cyber warfare units. It has a long way to go: to expel the United States from the Sea of China, it takes more than a few ships and planes. However, its neighbors are worried; Japan sees China's naval expansion as an existential threat that is forcing it to abandon its pacifism and increase its military power. For their part, Malaysia, the Philippines, Singapore and Vietnam feel threatened and are also increasing their military power. The greatest danger for its neighbors is that the Chinese leadership may try to alleviate its internal tensions by intensifying the aggression against neighboring countries and the United States.

China has been more restrained than Russia in its aggressions: harassment of Philippine warships, shipping oil rigs in waters claimed by Vietnam and China, claiming land and challenging possession of islands and reefs; and the establishment in 2013 of the so-called air defense identification zone - air space where China reserves the right to exclude foreign fighter aircraft in the East China Sea. This calculated aggression is a subtle form of the Russian strategy of hybrid forces. These actions have caused few military casualties and none of civilians, in a way that has forced the United States to act with caution, fearing that its response is exaggerated.

The Sea of China

The China Sea is located in East and Southeast Asia, with an extension of 4,250.00 km2. For practical purposes it is divided into: East China Sea and South China Sea. The latter is four times more extensive than the first.

East China Sea

Its limits are:

1. East: Japanese islands of Kyūshū and the archipelago of the Ryukyu Islands

2. West: Mainland China

3. North: Yellow Sea

4. South: island of Taiwan

5. Connected with the South China Sea by the Taiwan Strait and with the Sea of Japan by the Strait of Korea.

6. Its banks are part of South Korea, Taiwan and Mainland China, from the north and clockwise.

7. Drained rivers: Yangtze River (6,500 km).

8. Nearby Seas: South China Sea, Yellow Sea, Sea of Japan and Philippine.

9. Sea Inland islands: Gotō and Senkaku islands (JAP).

10. Cities: Shanghai, Hangzhou, Ningbo, Wenzhou and Fuzhou (CHN); Nagasaki and Akune (JAP); Taipei (TAI).

11. Gulfs and Bays: Hangzhou Bays, Sanmen and Funing.

12. Narrows: Strait of Korea (Sea of Japan); Strait of Taiwan, South China Sea.

13. Peninsula: Korean peninsula.

The Senkaku Islands

The Senkaku Islands are a small number of islands and cliffs (8 islands and many cliffs) that are under the administration of Japan but are claimed by the Republic of China (Taiwan) and the People's Republic of China as part of their claims about Taiwan. The origin of the dispute is in the existence of hydrocarbons in the area, in addition to the fishery resources that may have. They are situated on the edge of the continental shelf of Asia, and separated from the Ryukyu Islands by the Okinawa Depression. They are located 140 kilometers from the islet of Pengja, Taiwan, and 170 kilometers from the island of Ishigak (Japan). The largest is the island of Uotsuri-jima, made of stoneware and surrounded by a surface of coral. It has a hydrographic network constituted by seven small fountains and streams whose availability of fresh water is not enough to maintain a large human group.

The South China Sea

The South China Sea is the part of the Pacific Ocean bordering Brunei, Cambodia, China, Indonesia, Malaysia, Philippines, Singapore, Taiwan, Thailand and Vietnam. Its extension is of approximately 3. 500.000 km², and it extend from Singapore to Strait of Taiwan. It is also known as China Sea, South China Sea or Philippine Sea.

Its limits are:

1. East: Philippines

2. West: Cambodia, Indonesia, Thailand Vietnam

3. North: China, Hong Kong, Macao, Taiwan and Vietnam

4. South: Malaysia, Brunei, Indonesia and Singapore

5. Drained rivers: Pearl River, 2.00 km; Min River and Jiulon River (CHN); Red River, 1,149 km; Mekong River; River Rajang (MAL) and Pasing River (FIL).

6. Islands: The islands of the South China Sea form an archipelago of more than 200 uninhabited islands, banks, reefs, banks, reefs and sandbanks that are only conserved on the surface of the sea during the low tide or remain submerged in form permanent. The islands are grouped into three archipelagos, one bank and one bass. Together they have an area of less than 15 kilometers at low tide which includes:

   a. The Spratly Islands disputed by People's Republic of China, the Republic of China and Vietnam; Malaysia, Brunei and the Philippines claim a part of the archipelago.

   b. The Paracelsus Islands, disputed by the People's Republic of China, the Republic of China and occupied by the People's Republic of China.

   c. The Silver Islands, disputed by the People's Republic of China and the Republic of China, and occupied by the Republic of China (Taiwan).

   d. The MacLesfield Bank, disputed by the People's Republic of China, the Republic of China, the

Philippines and Vietnam, with no land above the sea surface.

e. The Masinloc or Scarborough Basin, disputed by the People's Republic of China, the Philippines and the Republic of China, with only rocks above sea level.

7. Straits: Strait of Luzon (Pacific Ocean); Strait of Taiwan (East China Sea); Straits of Mindoro and Balaba (Zulu Sea); Strait of Laut Natuna (Java Sea).

The China Sea has become the area with the largest influx of marine traffic on the planet. Twelve of the twenty most affluent ports are there: 1 in Singapore, 8 in China, 1 in Taiwan, 1 in South Korea and 1 in Malaysia. This saturation reveals the importance, dynamism and potential of this area. But it also reveals the risks and difficulties for maritime traffic and international relations. The confluence of so many boats in this small space, when compared with the volume of traffic, necessitates the existence of a control entity that avoids the inconveniences that are present. Only an agreement between the countries that benefit from these waters could give solution to a problem that gets more complicated each year. But it is at this point that the interests of a different order, especially the geopolitical ones, begin to converge. The hegemonic power, the United States, wants to maintain control of this area of the planet and free transit for its merchant and war ships. The emerging one, China, claims exactly the same thing; hence its claim on 80% of the surface of the South China Sea. Whoever controls the Sea of China will control the Asia-Pacific region; is not, then, a small matter. If China really wants to assume the role of superpower, it must start by controlling the seas that surround its continental territory. So that, although his claim on almost all the extension of the sea in question seems a legal exaggeration , but, from the geopolitical point of view has the support that gives the force. This difference of criteria, or desires, can generate, in the medium term, a warlike conflict between China and the United States. Surely none will give his arm to twist; will begin by reinforcing their military presence in the area, and will end up engaging in combat. This fact will not happen until China reaches the rank of superpower; despite the current growth of its economy, its income is not enough to put together a military apparatus with which it can confront the United States. If you try, what will happen to the Soviet Union will disappear without a trace. The fragility of a state whose growth has been based on the exploitation of comparative advantages that do not allow it to move the path of global competitiveness, not only in commercial terms, but also in the Geopolitical.

Disputes in the South China Sea

China claims 80% of the South China Sea (3.3 million km2), without taking into account the rights of coastal States: Vietnam, Taiwan, the Philippines, Brunei and Malaysia. This action is also affecting the interests of the country that for decades has been the guarantor of peace in that region: the United States. The international maritime laws recognize that each island generates rights in the 370 kilometers of the waters that surround it and on the resources that exist in its territory as well as in the bottom of the sea. The existence of abundant resources, minerals and fishery, explains the reason of the disputes for the possession of islands that in many cases are nothing more than rocks that hardly protrude from the surface of the sea.

Philippines demand

China has been building artificial expanses by the accumulation of sand in the middle of the South China Sea; The Philippines claims that what is present there are only islets, reefs and uninhabited rocks that generate only 12 miles of exclusion, while the Chinese claim that they are islands and therefore correspond to 200 miles. In January 2013, the Philippines sued China before the International Court of Arbitration in The Hague for violating international law, interfering with fishing, endangering maritime traffic and not protecting the environment. In July 2016, the Permanent Court of Arbitration in The Hague found no basis for China's territorial claims in the South China Sea and decided that it could not aspire to have rights over the exclusive economic zone in the area of the islands Spratly; there is no historical evidence, as stated in the ruling, that China has ever exercised exclusive control over the waters of the South China

Sea. In addition, the Court pointed out that China violated Philippine sovereignty and caused serious damage to coral reefs by practicing coral reef construction and affected endangered marine species. The Chinese government responded in a statement from its Foreign Ministry that the decision is unfounded, illegitimate, invalid and non-binding, and does not accept or acknowledge it. To back up this statement, China added a guided missile destroyer to the four who have been patrolling the area for the past two years. The United States reinforced its presence with a destroyer that joins the two who were already patrolling the area.

Dispute for the Paracelsus Islands

The Paracels Islands are a group of islands located in front of the island of Hainan whose tropical climate exposes them to typhoons that lash it between May and November of each year. Although surrounded by fishing areas and potential reserves of oil and gas, they lack natural resources of their own. China, Taiwan and Vietnam dispute their sovereignty. Its administration is in charge of the province of Hainan, People's Republic of China, as one of the first special economic zones. This is also being claimed by Taiwan and the Socialist Republic of Vietnam, although China, since 1974, de facto controls the Archipelago even though the International Community has not recognized its sovereignty over these islands.

The two Chinese

At the end of the Chinese civil war (1945-1949), the

nationalists, losing side, flee to the island of Taiwan and make up a new state (Republic of China). In the continent, the winners, communists, constitute the People's Republic of China that begins its management ignoring the state formed by its adversaries. Most of the States of the United Nations (UN) do not know Taiwan as a State, only 22 countries: 12 Latin American, 3 African, 1 European (Holy See) and 6 islands of Oceania. China, for its part, claims Taiwan as part of its territory.

Aggression and harassment

In general, it is possible to affirm that China is carrying out, in the Chinese Sea, an aggressive policy that is sustained, in the short and medium term, in the different territorial claims on islands and archipelagos, the ignorance of the related decisions with ongoing disputes and increasing naval power in the region. In the long term, the country's policy in the region is directed towards the expulsion of foreign naval forces and the control of naval, merchant and military traffic. China's growth over the past three decades has led its leadership to extend its influence beyond its borders. The China Sea is its first priority. But a strategy based on coercion and intimidation of its neighbors is creating tensions that could lead to an armed confrontation in the medium term. On the one hand, this country has been building artificial islands that serve as a basis for its territorial and maritime claims. In addition, it has been establishing bilateral agreements with countries in the region to allow the use of its port facilities in the Indian and Pacific Oceans, and to create a chain of protection that has been called: Pearl Necklace, designed to guarantee the safety of Its maritime supply lines to the Middle East and the freedom of action of its Navy.

This strategy consists of a containment chain made up of Chinese naval bases located in the Indian and Pacific oceans and ports and logistics facilities leased to allied countries located in the same maritime areas. It extends from the Indian Ocean, including the Red Sea, to the western end of the South China Sea. It includes the construction of a port in the Seychelles, as well as financing for the construction or improvement of others in Pakistan, Sri Lanka, Bangladesh and Myanmar. Its purpose is to counteract the United States' naval strategy (Sea Rings Strategy) and its new version, the Maritime Security Strategy for the Asia-Pacific Region. Also, it has been developing systems of weapons of denial of area —Anti-Access / Area Denial (A2 / AD), is its denomination in English— and deploying naval means, military and civil.

Chinese Geopolitics in Eurasia

The pivotal point of China's geopolitics in Eurasia is the Silk Road; let us begin, therefore, to define the limits of this vast portion of the planet. To enter, then, in the details that concern such an ambitious project. Eurasia is the space domain that includes the territory between European Russia and Asia. It is bordered by the Atlantic Ocean, the west, the Pacific Ocean, the east, the Arctic Ocean to the north, and by Africa, the

Mediterranean Sea and the Indian Ocean to the south. It covers 55 million square kilometers, 36% of the territory of planet Earth. It inhabits five billion people, 70% of the human population. In most of the treaties and conventions subscribed by Russia, the territorial space they cover extends only to Central Asia. Central Asia is a region that extends from the Caspian Sea to the borders of China, and from Russia to South Asia. For the UN, it comprises five ex-Soviet republics: Kazakhstan, Kyrgyzstan, Tajikistan, Turkmenistan and Uzbekistan. Sometimes it includes Mongolia, Afghanistan, North Pakistan, Northeastern Iran, Northwest India and West China. It can also include, depending on the context in which you want to use it, Inner Mongolia, southern Siberia and some Chinese provinces such as Qinghai, Tibet and Gansu. This region is sometimes called Turkestan.

The Silk Road

The objective of the Chinese Silk Road project is to sponsor economic cooperation in Eurasia by investing in infrastructure for roads, railways, airports and ports that will connect China with Russia, Africa, Europe and Oceania, will increase China's influence and affect Russia's expansion plans to Central Asia. The land silk route will begin in western China and will traverse it as a whole. Its center will be the capital of XinJiang province. From Ürümqi it will connect with Kazakhstan, Kyrgyzstan, Uzbekistan, and even Afghanistan and Iran. From Turkey you can reach Russia and Europe. Among the projects is a high-speed train from Bulgaria to Xinxiang province. Another one of these trains will connect Moscow with Beijing, in a route of 7,000 kilometers. A third railway route will link Laos, Thailand, Malaysia and Singapore with China. In the first half of 2016, most contracts abroad have been made by China along the Silk Road. In February, Chinese group Cosco Limited bought 67% of the shares in the Port of Piraeus, the largest in Greece, for 368.5 million euros, payable in two parts. This company also committed to invest in that port for an amount of 350 million euros. Other Chinese companies are building a high-speed rail network that will link that city with Hungary and Germany. The construction of the third stage of a nuclear reactor in Pakistan should commence by July 2016; in addition, $ 2 trillion was invested in a coal mine in the Thar Desert.

The Silk Road is a strategic project involving more than 60 countries, corresponding to China's economic expansion plans and its desire to become a power that extends its influence in a peaceful and moderate manner. This expansion will involve Europe, Eurasia and China, and will exclude the United States. China has already reported on 900 projects underway, valued at 890 billion dollars, out of a total of four trillion dollars of investment in the medium term. The financial structure that will support it is taking shape. In 2015, the Central Bank of China transferred $ 82 trillion to three state banks to finance projects on the Silk Road. A $ 40 trillion sovereign fund was also created; in addition, the Asian Infrastructure Investment Bank

(AIIB) was endowed with a fund of 100 billion dollars to support all projects associated with said route. The Asian Infrastructure Investment Bank (AIIB) is a multilateral institution with 57 members. The main shareholder is the government of China. The rest of China is mobilizing around the Route; two-thirds of its provinces have emphasized the importance of this project for its development. Fujian province has established a free trade zone to attract Southeast Asian companies. Most Chinese state-owned enterprises already have a department that deals with this commercial corridor. Foreign direct investment (FDI) has been increasing along this trade path and is growing twice as fast as in the rest of the country. In the first half of 2016 the FDI of the Route represented 52% of such investment. The Chinese bureaucracy sees in the Silk Road an opportunity to reduce dependence on domestic investment in infrastructure to maintain the pace of economic growth. In addition, he thinks it could serve as an outlet for the surpluses that have accumulated its state-owned enterprises, especially steel and cement. To carry out a project of this magnitude, China needs raw materials and energy in abundance; it is there that Russia plays a fundamental role.

The alliance between China and Russia.

Both the Silk Road project and the presence of a common adversary, the United States, have brought two rivals from before. This camaraderie will continue as long as both acquire the necessary strength, especially the economic one, to take the place of the hegemonic power. In 2014, both countries signed the Joint Declaration on the New Stage of Global Action Relations and Strategic Cooperation, containing the bases for a stable and lasting relationship that would counteract the influence of the United States in the region, facilitate Russia strengthening its economy and providing China with access to the raw materials and energy it requires for the full development of its economic potential. But, the most important for both is the establishment of an alliance that will facilitate the construction of a new world order of multipolar character. According to a Foreign Affairs report, Russia has not, despite its intention, been able to increase investment in China, especially in the areas of its greatest interest, such as gas and oil. "The construction of two pipelines to bring Siberian gas to various regions of China has been postponed until 2020"[2]. The decline in oil and gas prices and sanctions imposed by the West has cast doubt on the profitability of the projects to exploit these products in eastern Siberia. In addition, Russia has been compelled to compete with supply from both traditional suppliers (Saudi Arabia and Southeast Asia) and third countries: Angola, Equatorial Guinea, Iraq, Turkmenistan, and, in a short time, once Sanctions are lifted, Iran.

In terms of armaments, China's demand has dropped by a trillion dollars a year, as China is developing its own military industry and has reached third place as a global exporter of armaments. However, Russia remains its main supplier of aviation engines, radars, naval weapons and missile components. To increase the competitiveness of its offer, Russia has offered China its most sophisticated arsenal: Sukhoi Su-35 fighter jets and S-400 ground-to-air missiles. In financial matters, China has become the main borrower of Russia. In 2014, the amount of money supplied to the Russians to finance bilateral trade amounted to 11.6 trillion dollars. However, China's offer has not offset the decline in financial resources coming from Western banks: "Since 2066, China's direct investment in Russia has gradually declined. Both countries failed to reach the $ 100 trillion target for trade, by a long stretch, reaching only $ 64.2 trillion[3.]

China's financial dependence is affecting Russia's intention to exert a preponderant influence in Central Asia. It has been forced to accept Chinese projects that affect its interests in that region. Such is the case of the Chinese project of the Silk Road. President Vladimir Putin himself admitted after a meeting with Chinese President Xi Jinping in May 2015 that: "The Silk Road Project will force Russia to cede much more political power in Asia Central and accept greater dependence on China "[4].

Due to the sanctions that prevent Russian companies from accessing financial markets, Russia is increasingly increasing its dependence on Chinese capital. Gazprom, a natural gas company, obtained a $ 2 trillion loan from the Bank of China; Rosneft, a state-owned oil company, has received $ 35 billion over the past three years in oil-payable loans. Despite this dependence, the volume of Chinese exports to Russia fell by 34% in 2015; while China's imports from Russia have fallen by 19% since 2009. The economic difficulties facing both countries suggest an even greater decline in trade and financial exchange in the coming years. China has signed 43 trade agreements with Russia, estimated to reach about $ 200 billion by 2020, including:

1. Extension of the Moscow Metro, with an investment of 1700 million dollars.
2. Installation of a car factory in Tula, with an investment of 500 million dollars.
3. Assignment by Russia of technology for the construction of commercial aircraft similar to Airbus and Boeing.
4. Cooperation in space matters.
5. Supply of Russian aircraft and submarines to China.
6. China's participation in the exploitation of the Udorav copper mine.
7. Russian gas supply to China for 30 years.
8. Russian oil supplies to China for 20 years.

Western sanctions have isolated the Russian economy from the global context, and China is seizing this opportunity to unite the resources of the Russian distant with its industrial northeast in an area of economic integration geared to its industrial development priorities. Russia's sovereignty over its eastern territories and its influence over Eurasia and Central Asia are being eroded. As its economic dependence on China increases, Russia will have fewer opportunities to regain its global power status.

Economic sanctions on Russia are having a counterparty effect expected by the West, as it is giving China the opportunity to increase its economic and political influence over Eurasia and Central Asia in a shorter time than anticipated in its expansion plans. The current state of Sino-Russian relations does not provide any geopolitical advantage to Russia vis-à-vis the European Community, as it has diversified its exports, attracted new investments, and increased trade with China, with a growth of more than 500 trillion dollars in recent years. So that, as the ties between Russia and China weaken, the Sino-Europeans are strengthened.

Despite the efforts of his government, the importance of Russia in the global political scenario is weakening, the preponderance will be in the near future in the hands of third parties, be it China or the Western Bloc. If this trend continues, China will take the leadership of all Eurasia and Russia will have to settle for a secondary and irrelevant role.

Geopolitics of China in the Indian Subcontinent

The Indian subcontinent is divided, from the geographical point of view, into four parts:

1. The mountainous framework that stretches from the Arabian Sea to the Bay of Bengal.

39

2. The North India Plain, stretching from southeast Delhi through the Ganges River delta to the border of Myanmar, and the Himalayas in the north to the southern hills.

3. The Indian peninsula that goes south in the Indian Ocean and consists of a variety of terrain but mainly mountainous;

4. The deserts in the west between the North Indian Plain and the Indus River Valley of Pakistan.

The countries that are part of this subcontinent are:

India which is located north of the equator and extends from north latitude 8 ° 4 'and 37 ° 6' and longitude 68 ° 7 'to 97 ° 25'. It limits the north with Nepal and Bhutan; To the south with the Strait of Palk and the Gulf of Mannar, separating it from Sri Lanka and the Indian Ocean; To the west with the Arabian Sea and Pakistan; To the east with Burma, the Gulf of Bengal and Bangladesh, which almost completely separates northwest India from the rest of the country. Officially named Bharat Ganarajiyá (Republic of India, in Hindi), is a member of the Commonwealth. Together with the Jammu and Kashmir regions (whose definitive legal-territorial status has not yet been determined), India has an area of 3,165,596 km². Its capital is New Delhi and the largest city Mumbai.

Pakistan occupies the western region of the sub-continent and extends around the Indus Valley. It is separated from India itself by an impassable desert and by marshes in the south, leaving only Punjab in the central part of the country as a point of contact.

Bangladesh is located in the Ganges River Delta; Most of its territory is below sea level and is therefore very vulnerable to flooding from the Bay of Bengal.

The kingdoms of Nepal and Bhutan are located on the heights of the Himalayas, on the edge of the subcontinent. There is a small corridor between Nepal and Bangladesh that interconnects with the northeastern region of India and the eastern border of India with Myanmar. From the territorial division between India and Pakistan, the conflict begins by the possession of the Kashmir region. India seeks as allies to the United Kingdom and Russia; Pakistan is supported by the United States and the People's Republic of China. In the time of the sixties China and India face in a war in which, finally, the second one loses the territory of Aksai Chin, region of Ladak. From that moment, the Effective Control Line, or Linea McCartney-McDonald, was constituted in the unofficial border between both countries.

India and China

Between China and India there is an insurmountable natural barrier: the Himalayan ridge. A warlike confrontation between them on that side is unlikely: their terrestrial interconnection is possible only through very narrow steps. At sea, the situation is different; both are fighting for control of the

Indian Ocean sea routes. The Chinese strategy of the Pearl Necklace threatens the flow of natural resources to India and affects the freedom of navigation of its naval fleet. The projection of Chinese influence in countries bordering the Indian Ocean —Kenya, Pakistan, Sri Lanka, Bangladesh and Myanmar— worries India. To counter China's strategy, India has been tightening ties with the United States and strengthening its military power. Two events have recently been set to mark its true intention: the successful test of its 5,000-kilometer-wide Agni V ballistic missile and the inauguration of the ten-year Russian-made nuclear submarine INS Chakra, Akula II class, nomenclature of the NATO. In space, satellites in India watch over China and their naval fleet sails through the South China Sea.

III MARX VS. SMITH

The technical gap

China is the only country on the planet with the potential to compete with the United States and become the hegemonic power. However, its technological lag makes this option difficult. In general, the problems that most affect China are: the deceleration of its economy, excessive environmental pollution, widespread corruption, the absence of a social security system, financial markets with little transparency and recognized inefficiency, demographic aging and an impatient middle class. But, the biggest difficulty is its low level of technology, compared to the United States. While China exports a considerable volume of high-tech goods, half of these correspond to the assembly of goods commissioned by foreign companies: parts are imported, assembled and returned to the contractor. Measured in terms of GDP, it seems that the Chinese economy is on the heels of the North American; but this index is misleading because it only represents a periodic cut that does not reflect the economic spectrum in its entirety. A new way of measuring the degree of development of an economy is the method that has been given the name of the Inclusive Wealth

Index (IRI), a project that includes institutions such as the UN University and the Environment Program Environment (UNEP), and which accounts for the assets of a country in three areas:

1. Manufactured capital: infrastructure, facilities, machinery and equipment.
2. Human Capital: competencies, education and health.
3. Natural Capital: subsoil resources, ecosystem and atmosphere.

To measure this index, 20 countries, representing 56% of the world's population and 72% of world GDP, have been selected in the period 1990 to 2008. These countries are: Australia, Brazil, Canada, Chile, China, Colombia, Ecuador, France, Germany, India, Japan, Kenya, Nigeria, Norway, Russia, Saudi Arabia, South Africa, USA, United Kingdom and Venezuela. Using this method, the US measurement reaches 144 trillion dollars, while China only reaches 32 trillion, being therefore 4, 5 times less: an unreachable gap, since the former invests 10 times more in research and development than the second. The apparent economic parity between the two countries is therefore no longer a myth, and the rise of China to a hegemonic position in the international context is an unattainable dream.

Economy of China today

In the Year 2015, Chinese GDP reached 7.4%, the lowest in the last 25 years. Paul Krugman, Nobel laureate in Economics 2008, argues that the question is not whether the Chinese economy will collapse, but when: "The Chinese century is not the beginning of the end, it is the end of the beginning"[1].The principle was spectacular, China's Gross Domestic Product (GDP) grew between 1978 and 2011 an average of 10% annually, over those 33 years. The most optimistic economic predictions projected that China would surpass the United States between 2010 and 2014; the most pessimistic set 2019 for this to happen. The slowdown in recent years has postponed this forecast. Until the time of the world financial crisis, September 2008, the biggest problem of the Chinese economy was the debt of local governments. This has passed into the background.

The financial issues that overwhelm the authorities of this Asian country have two aspects that are closely interconnected. In the first place is the corporate debt, in the second is that of an unstable and improvised capital market. Chinese corporate debt has grown disproportionately in the last ten years, from a healthy 50% to 260% of the Gross Domestic Product (GDP). Loans with problems have multiplied by two in the last two years. Almost 2/5 of the new debt is used to pay interest on the existing debt; 16% of the 1000 largest companies owe more in interest than they earn before taxes. The country needs more and more credit to produce less and less growth: 4 Yuan of loans are needed to generate one Yuan of additional GDP growth; before the 2008 crisis the ratio was 1x1.

While, overall, China is a net creditor, the biggest problem is inside. The Chinese state owns the largest banks; its largest creditors, the gigantic and oversized state-owned enterprises, also belong to the State. Their competitive inability forces them to survive at the expense of public money; its debt is expanding at a rate that is double the growth of the economy. In September 2015 Zhang Xiwu, deputy chairman of the State Assets Supervision Commission, explained to the social media, without questions, an outline of a reform plan —consisting of three parts and a total of eight chapters— whose elaboration was attributed to the Central Committee of the Communist Party (PCCH) and the Council of State. According to this document, China will modernize its state-owned enterprises and promote mixed ownership and private capital inflows, so that they can have the independence and responsibility necessary to make profits and take on losses and risks as well as face international rivals. This plan will affect 150,000 state-owned enterprises, with assets of 15.69 trillion dollars and 30 million workers on their payroll.

These companies will be divided into two categories: those of benefits, with a market approach, and those dedicated to the public welfare. It is also provided that the state banks provide the money necessary for the planned conversion. Despite the time elapsed, this initiative has not materialized with the speed with which the current economic situation requires. . And, we doubt very much that someday comes true, because what has appeared is a struggle between the progressive sector and the conservative PCCH. In addition, the liquidity problems that are occurring in public banks have prevented government banks from providing the promised capital.

Another option is the domestic capital market; But this does not count with the maturity and reliability required

by private partners. The option of external markets is less viable; China's legislation provides neither the security nor the protection demanded by foreign investors; to make matters worse, the Chinese judicial system is venal and corrupt.

Transactions by banks in the shade are worsening the internal financial situation. Unlike the current global financial legislation, reformulated after the 2008 crisis, in which the activities of conventional banks and banks are separated in the shade, and expressly forbids the former to carry out activities that concern the second, In China traditional banking can act on both fronts. In the first, it offers the guarantees of rigor to its savers; in the second there is no protection.

Despite this difference in the handling of transactions between the two types of banks, Chinese savers invest their money in financial adventures that could volatilize their money and expose them to scams and Ponzi scheme. To obtain money, Chinese banks sell a product called the Wealth Management Product (WMP). It shares some characteristics of instruments that were common in the US market prior to the 2008 crisis and were used to deceive US investors: the Collateralized Debt Obligations (CDOs) and the Collaborative Investment Instruments (SIVs). This Chinese financial instrument is based

47

on the Investor Reserve Fund (FRI), whose money is obtained through the sale of the WMP. From there it is invested in a variety of assets that are located along the spectrum of financial risk. One party to reliable products and others to higher risk interbank lending, although the facts suggest that they are in fact high risking most cases, investors are the same customers as banks, who transfer their money from their savings accounts to the WMPs of their own bank. When the deadline expires the bank expects its customers to immediately buy new WMPs and keep the flow of money.

WMPs have an insurmountable shortfall: a maturity shorter than the assets in which the money is invested, and which on average is 113 days. Once they expire, the money returns to the investor's savings account. The current trend is to reinvest, but, over time, a vicious circle can be formed that distorts the market. If savers lose, as will sooner or later, their confidence in this type of financial instrument, the flow of money will decrease considerably, the bank will have liquidity problems, and all this financial apparatus will go to a pit.

In large banks, WMPs account for only 15% of deposits. In the middle 40%, and any difficulty can cause serious damage to the generator of the product. The scarce investment opportunities in the Chinese financial market, the very low interest rates offered to savers, and the slowdown in economic activity are increasing the demand for the products in question. Ended, medium-sized banks have been the most aggressive, and often evading regulations in force, they have been placing their clients' money in companies that are asking for money not to leverage their growth plans but to get out of the financial difficulties caused for its inefficiency and low competitiveness. The bulk of the investments are being made in the most difficult companies in sectors such as insurers, port-to-port (P2P) lenders and risk management (especially junk bonds), among others. A quote from The Economics Magazine, May 7, 2016, explains the current situation:

> This is a vicious circle. Savers show an insatiable appetite for these products and banks are induced to create even more. As a result they sink deeper into the shadows, far enough away from conventional banking to offer higher rates, but close enough to their customers who maintain their confidence in banks and their risk products. This situation has extended the hidden risks in the Chinese economy[2].

What Chinese banking is doing in the shadow is more like the roulette game (the Russian one would say) than a financial activity; if this continues the Chinese economy will sink and drag with the rest of the world banking. Despite the economic slowdown, state-owned companies continue to demand money to run the wrinkle, waiting for better times, so the state provides money to the public bank to maintain both liquidity and credit. This money is almost never targeted at competitive businesses, the greater portion of the money goes to those in difficulty. Of course private companies do not receive the money they require to maintain their activity. Chinese banks are currently short of capital, as they lend 100% of what they receive from their savers and leave no reserve. In spite of this situation, the demands of the public banks for obtaining credits are becoming smaller and each day is greater the insolvency.

According to official figures, of the two hundred billion dollars (US $ 200 B) contributed to balance the capital market, 65 billion have become bad credits. To disguise this problem, the banks do not declare the moratorium, and they change that denomination by the one of expired, but not demandable. There is evidence that the situation in this market is even worse than the government figures indicate, since a good part of the money obtained is stolen or wasted.

The Chinese capital market is in its infancy, as it presents many shortcomings, among which are:

-Corruption
- Price manipulation
-Government intervention
-Limited legal protection for investors
-Small surveillance by the control institutions

In China, there are few companies that capitalize through the capital market; prefer to get money by means of loans. For many, this market functions like a casino, as there are few rules that control its operation, and those that exist often are overlooked. The service of foreign credit rating agencies (Moody, s, S & P and Fitch, among others) is not used; Chinese agencies of little credibility are used. 80% of the transactions are handled by retail investors of dubious reputation and limited experience. Older investors also do not act honestly

and prefer short-term transactions: they buy today to sell tomorrow. It is difficult for insurers to act in a market with these characteristics, as their business is only viable in the long term.

Despite these difficulties, the capital market grew explosively in 2015. It rose from 7.7 trillion Yuan in 2014 to 12.5 trillion Yuan in that year. To a large extent this abrupt growth is due to repurchase. Companies buy their own shares and apply for credit based on these assets; with this money they acquire more actions and so on. This game will end when the market crashes. International banking that participates in the Chinese market has only 1.5% of commercial banking assets. In most cases their clients are foreign investors who do not dare to put their money in the hands of the Chinese.

A colossus with crystal slippers

Some analysts think that China could replace the United States in the medium term as the world's first economy. We are of the opposite opinion, neither is it so easy nor takes so little time. The economic power of the United States is based on the ability of its private companies to dominate the business world-wide. Chinese companies do not have that capability. The largest and most powerful belong to the State and depend on investment and official protection. They are concentrated in the domestic market and are unable to face the competition of the foreign ones.

Western companies dominate the market for high-tech goods and services; companies such as Google, Microsoft, Samsung and Apple, among others, control world trade, and the Chinese alone can compete with those in their domestic market, thanks to restrictions imposed by local authorities.

China's economic growth continues today to depend on the localization of production of foreign enterprises that take advantage of the low wages of a labor mass without specialization or qualification. Despite the fact that manufacturers have been simplifying their manufacturing processes to reduce costs, the considerable increase in wages in recent years is making that comparative advantage disappear.

China does not have companies that can compete in the manufacture of capital goods (goods that are used to produce other goods). Nor has it developed capacity to create and sell sophisticated goods such as semiconductors, nuclear reactors, offshore wind turbines and commercial aircraft of the size of those produced by Boeing, USA, or Airbus, European Community. Its ability to operate in medium-technology markets continues to depend on a limited range of products, that include automotive vehicles, computers, , high-speed rail systems telecommunications equipment, and agricultural machinery, power generation equipment, ground-based wind turbines among others.

The economic indicator figures can be misleading and disguise the reality: a higher percentage in the Gross Domestic Product (GDP), volume of cargo and amount of monetary reserves does not necessarily mean that China is dominating the spectrum of the world economy. Let us take the following example: in spite of the fact that in the volume of maritime cargo China continues to lead the world trade with a percentage that fluctuates between 50 and 70% of the total of containers, the value of the property of the remaining percentage exceeds that by far.

Most of China's productive capacity is oriented towards the manufacture of downstream goods through the use of imported technology, simplification of manufacturing processes and adaptation of advanced designs to manufacture more basic goods that have a lower cost. . While, on the one hand, they meet the needs of less demanding customers, on the other hand they inhibit the manufacture of goods for customers who demand high quality and high technology objects. By contrast, Western companies focus on sophisticated, upstream products that target the needs of a small and select number of customers. This type of company designs high-performance products —incorporating new technologies and advanced software— and distributes them through global supply chains. In this way the West has managed to dominate the market for nuclear plants, robotics industry and advance combat aircraft. It is not clear how China will overcome this gap and change the direction of its production system. Despite the fact that China has been penetrating markets that were once exclusive to Western companies, Latin America and Africa, among others, the volume of its exports depends on the generosity of loans the Chinese government gives to its new trading partners. In these markets, China has acted with some naivety and, in some cases, that exchange has left only a huge and unpayable debt; is the case of Venezuela whose government requested in June 2016 that the Chinese declare a moratorium on the $ 65 billion of debt accumulated in the last decade.

A significant shortfall in Chinese production is that it is self-sufficient and does not take advantage of the global supply chains. For example, when it comes to making critical components, such as jet aircraft avionics, a learning process is initiated that allows building it at home and avoiding its importation. Western companies act differently; simply look for the manufacturer, anywhere in the world, who can supply the product that meets its needs and technical requirements. Even in the domestic market, China is at a disadvantage when it comes to products that rely heavily on investment in marketing and research and development (R & D). According to Ghemawat And Hout:

> Foreign companies operating in China lead in 10 of the 13 industries in which R & D costs more than 6% of revenues, including jet, software and semiconductor aircraft. Also in 4 of the 6 industries in which the cost of advertising exceeds 6% of revenues, including carbonated beverages, patented

pharmaceuticals and daily care and beauty articles[3].

Chinese companies are highly dependent on Western technology. Although much money has been invested in education, research and entrepreneurship in recent years, little has been invested in improving what really matters: freedom of thought and free will. No one can be creative in an environment where individual rights are curtailed. No matter how much money is invested, genius ideas, such as those that underpin entrepreneurship in the West, only arise when the spirit feels free.

We are of the opinion that China reached as far as its limitations allowed. From now on, only the decline can be expected. It will never reach the status of the world's leading power. Unless his current political regime changes; the ideological muzzle of the Chinese Communist Party is an insurmountable obstacle. In Democracy they could have the Chinese a better chance, however, a lot of time will have to happen. For us, China is nothing more than a colossus with crystal slippers.

The Financial Laboratory

Since Hong Kong became part of China, its status as a global financial center has been exploited by the central government as a kind of laboratory where communist leaders learn how a capitalist economy really works. The transition of this country towards a hegemonic position in the global scenario passes through the adoption of the habits of the market. So far the Chinese leadership has not resisted the temptation to manipulate macroeconomic variables every time a crisis occurs. But, on the other hand, financial markets are relying less and less on the figures offered by the Central Bank of China and the Yuan has failed to position itself as the global currency of financial exchange. In this way, China will neither succeed in overcoming the problems of its economy nor will it transform itself into a global power that moves the United States from its privileged position.

Hong Kong has its own currency, institutions and laws. The Hong Kong dollar has been linked to the US for 32 years. Only 11% of Hong Kong's bank deposits are in Chinese currency and bonds are traded at prices that differ from those offered by the Shanghai Stock Exchange. Hong Kong's main bank, HSBC, is headquartered in London. The businessmen of this financial enclave prefer to do business with the West and distrust China's financial authorities. In the financial market of Hong Kong is where the contradictions of the Chinese economy can best be appreciated. This forms an incoherent totality that is open in some cases and closed in others, as referred to in an article in The Economics:

> Foreigners can build factories but not buy bonds. Chinese companies are second in cross-border investment, measured by the stock of their direct investment, but their market for private funds is irrelevant: three streets in Edinburgh are home to

more international assets. Continental consumers can buy BMW cars and Gucci wallets but cannot buy shares of those companies. China's Central Bank (along with its related agencies) is perhaps the largest buyer in the world in the most transparent bond markets, but it is, in turn, as opaque as the Huangpu River. State banks lend like lions in Africa, but they are shy as mice in Western capital markets. When China shudders, the price of oil falls, but oil contracts of derivatives are traded elsewhere[4].

For China to overcome these contradictions, it must solve, first of all, the greatest of these: a political model that is not compatible with the capitalist system. If anything have served these thirty years of the Chinese experiment is to understand that without individual freedom there is no free market. The double standard with which China has oriented its economic expansion is already exhausted, there is no way to correct the deficiencies that it has accumulated during three decades. There is no economic or financial solution available to correct the defects that have accumulated in that period; if China does not open itself to free will, its economy will sink into its own contradictions. And if its economy collapses, the dream of becoming the hegemonic power will also fade away.

IV A TRUE COLOSSUS

United States and Asia-Pacific Region

After the beginning of World War II, the United States designed the Marine Rings Strategy, conceived in the year 1942, which consists of the formation of a ring that is based on three positions that serve as a hinge: The Bering Strait, The Persian Gulf and the Strait of Gibraltar. Its purpose was to inhibit the freedom of action of Eurasia throughout —including China, Europe and Russia— North Africa and India, to maintain the flow of world trade and, finally, to facilitate maritime patrolling by its naval fleet In the Indian and Pacific Oceans.

In order to address China's expansion strategy in the Asia-Pacific region, and in particular in the China Sea, the United States designed the Asia-Pacific Maritime Safety Strategy (ESMRAP) in 2015. The first part is an analysis of the strategic context, the second presents national objectives and the third proposes lines of effort to ensure maritime safety in the region. The analysis describes a region whose development has made it one of the most important at the global level, especially in the maritime sector, where an important part of the energy flow and the global container trade flows.

This document adds that threats of a military nature are

joined by other existing ones: illicit trafficking of all kinds, piracy and natural disasters. The origin of the territorial claims is placed by the analysis in the energy reserves and the fishing potential of the region. The United States, refers to the document in question, does not take a position on any of the territorial claims in progress, but expresses its desire for its peaceful settlement; however, is concerned that some of these claims are unaware of international agreements relating to the right to innocent passage and the development of military activities by third States in the Economic Exclusion Zones. The analysis considers that China's claims do not conform to international law and expressly condemn the declaration of Air Defense Identification Zones and the inappropriate use of the means of civilian maritime security agencies. There is also criticism of the growing use of non-military means with the intention of coercing third parties, dangerous maneuvers in air and sea navigation, especially by military means, territorial claims and the construction of artificial islands serving as starting point for a future strategic projection of Chinese military power.

Goals:

1. Safeguarding freedom in the international waters of the region.
2. Deterrence against attempts of coercion or conflict, by China.

3. Promotion of respect for international law and conventions.

Lines of effort:

1. Strengthening military capabilities in the region to help achieve a level of deterrence that prevents conflict development or enforcement and provides an effective response to any threat. This line is based on the development and modernization of capacities, the deployment of resources based on a better distribution of resources and capacities and the execution of exercises, either unilaterally or in combination with partners and allies.

2. Building partnerships and enhancing the capacities of the countries of the region to increase regional security capacities and raise awareness of the maritime environment to facilitate actions that respond to existing challenges.

3. Reduction of risk on the basis of two directions. The first, the definition of relations with China on the basis of cooperation and competition. The second focuses on measures to reduce risks through various mechanisms: meetings and common protocols of action.

4. Construction of a regional cooperation architecture that promotes international conventions and protocols, with special attention to the Association of Southeast Asian Nations (ASEAN) and its meeting of defense ministers.

In order to achieve the intended objectives, the United States has relocated 60% of its land and naval air capacity so that its employment is more operationally reliable and sustainable from the political point of view. In addition, it plans to modernize its war platform in South Korea and Japan (with emphasis on Okinawa), Australia, Guam (the focal point of its strategy in that area) and Hawaii, and place the best of its personnel and deploy its most sophisticated weapons, such as:

- Aviation: F-22 and F-35 aircraft (stealth); P-8A Poseidon (anti-submarine warfare, vessel interception and electronic warfare); Bomber B-2; V- 22 Ospreys (tilt-rotor aircraft capable of take-off and vertical landing and horizontal flight.

- Navy: Increase in the number of surface ships; Submarines of the class Virginia; Advanced antisubmarine drones; Aircraft strategic bomber B-21; and the most advanced in space technology, electronic warfare and cyber warfare.

It is also conducting training exercises with the participation of its allies, such as the RIM of the Pacific (RIMPAC), conducted in July 2016. This event is the largest of its kind and brought together 26 countries. China and the United States sailed together from Guam to Hawaii, and conducted joint exercises that included search and rescue. Japan, is receiving the help it needs to face China's arbitrariness, among the actions planned in the ESMRAP is: "United States in a wide range of contingencies, including those below the threshold of conflict and those related to space and cyberspace[2].

South Korea is another of the allies that is receiving special attention:

> In June 2016, as part of the North Korean ballistic missile defense effort, the two countries decided to deploy an advanced missile defense battery - the High Altitude Air Defense (THAAD) - in South Korean soil[3].

The Philippines is another important chip in strategic chess, so it receives support from the US to improve its operational readiness, in the form of: "Joint training to help the Philippines better defend itself and aid in modernizing its armed forces by Medium of the agreement to improve defense cooperation, signed in 2014 "[4].

Other countries in the region are receiving the collaboration of the United States government. In December 2015, Singapore and Singapore signed an agreement to improve defense cooperation; it was agreed to send a P-8A Poseidon aircraft and four ships for combat on the coast, within the force rotation program that is part of the ESMRAP. In May 2016, President Obama visited Vietnam to strengthen relations between the two countries and lift the ban on sales of deadly weapons. Indonesia and Malaysia were helped to improve their defensive capabilities. Australia received the attention deserved by an unconditional ally: "The US-Australia alliance is becoming more global; both countries have continued their close collaboration, not only across the region, but also outside the region, in the struggle for the defeat of the Islamic State (EI)"[5].

Outside the region, the United States focused its attention on a powerful and necessary ally: "In June 2016, the United States recognized India as one of its greatest allies for defense, to allow defense trade and technology exchange agreements at a level the United States reserves for its best allies"[6]. Four years ago, India and the United States signed the Defense Technology Trade Initiative to take advantage of the technological and industrial capabilities of both countries. Nowadays the agreement is already bearing fruit in a wide spectrum of defense products.

The realization of the ESMRAP is achieving an unwanted effect: the isolation of China from the regional context. A great part of the fault is that country, because with their actions they are erecting a barrier more effective than the Great Wall. While the rest of the countries are uniting to promote the political, economic and military development of the region, China is determined to assault its neighbors and to create an environment of tension that can lead the wrong way.

Military Bases of the United States

Most of the military bases of the United States were constructed after World War II, to contain the advance of the communism. At present, about 850 military installations can be counted in 76 countries. They are distributed in nine mayor commands:

1. Northern Command, Peterson Air Force Base, Colorado.
2. Pacific Command, Honolulu, Hawaii.
3. Southern Command, Miami, Florida.
4. Central Command, MacDill Air Force Base, Florida.
5. European Command, Stuttgart,- Vaihingen, Germany.
6. Joint Forces Command, Norfolk, Virginia, United States.
7. Special Operations Command, MacDill Air Force Base, Florida.
8. Transportation Command, Scott Air Force Base, Illinois.
9. Strategic Command, Offutt Air Force Base, Nebraska.

Anti-missile shield

The anti-missile system installed by the United States in Europe is intended to intercept missiles from North Korea and Iran. The Russians claim that this is a threat to their national

security that could undermine the stability of the region because it can be easily modified to launch medium-range missiles that destroy the control system of its strategic nuclear forces.

This system works according to the following sequence:

1. Launch of a hostile ballistic missile. Early warning satellites and radars detect, track enemy missiles and send information to the United States.
2. A high-definition radar X-band terrestrial base tracks missile and decoys.
3. One or more interceptor rockets are launched from a naval base.
4. The destroying vehicle identifies the warhead and decoys separately.
5. The destructive missile follows the warhead and destroys it.

The parts that make up the system are spread over different countries, for example: an early warning radar is in Turkey; A ground-based radar in X-band is in Romania; In the naval base of Rota, Spain, are ships capable of transporting ballistic missiles of defense; the central command is in Ramstein, Germany; and in space are the satellites of communications and surveillance.

Inclusive Wealth and Military Power

While the measurement of GDP only reaches an economic connotation due to the short reach of its projections, the Inclusive Wealth Index (IRI), on the other hand, can be used for strategic projections and the geopolitical positioning of a particular State.

In the last measurement it can be seen that the United States has more capacity than China to transform resources into economic and military power; and that its scientific and technological backwardness, even if its economic growth exceeds the current state, is an impediment that will considerably delay the materialization of its plans to transform itself into a superpower.

Time is another variable that plays against China. The United States has decades of transforming its wealth into a military power that allows it to operate globally to maintain control over the planet's space, air, land, and sea. Since World War II, it has been creating the infrastructure that allows it to master these areas. The systems that comprise it - from silent nuclear submarines, through fleets of aircraft carriers, to surveillance satellites - provide a superiority that will be unattainable by any of its adversaries.

The basis of US military power, and part of its IRI, is its massive scientific and industrial base. The clusters, which are developed around the best universities in the world, are the first instance. In this, the investment in research and development exceeds in about ten times the one of China, and contributes to that the technology gap between both expands more and more. Money is not an obstacle, for it flows freely through its sophisticated financial system, without the least participation of the state. Innovation and entrepreneurship also play an important role in this instance.

In the second instance is the complex network that manages the defense projects, which is made up of a combination of laboratories, research institutes, contractors and bureaucrats who interact in a harmonious way to concretize projects and provide the most sophisticated weapon systems of the world. The Chinese are very far from achieving this bureaucratic sophistication, say Brooks and Wohlforth who:

> China's defense industry is still in its infancy: apart from a few pockets of excellence, such as ballistic missiles, the Chinese industrial military complex has been shown to have few capabilities to design and produce advanced conventional weapons systems. For example, China is not yet capable of producing high-performance engines for fighter jets, despite the immense resources it has invested, and depends on second-rate Russian engines[7].

In relation to the Naval War, this Asian country does not come out very well either:

> China is poorly equipped for anti-submarine warfare and is doing little to improve; it is only now capable of producing silent nuclear submarines similar to those developed by the United States during World War II. Since then, this country has invested hundreds of thousands of dollars and six decades of effort in developing the current generation of silent submarines of the Virginia class that have absolute levels of silence[8].

Another aspect to consider is the infrastructure required for the use of different weapons systems:

> To employ them is difficult, not only because weapons tend to be complex, but also because they have to be used in a coordinated way. This is a very complex task, as in the case of the deployment of an aircraft carrier battle group; Media, ships and airplanes have to be put to work together in real

time. Drones, for example, work best when they have highly qualified personnel and the technological and organizational ability to quickly collect process and employ on the basis of information gained instantly on the battlefield[9].

China does not seem to have that capacity: "Developing the Necessary infrastructure could take a long time to military organization, and since this task requires high levels of decentralization, the hierarchical and centralized armed forces are inadequate to achieve this organizational capacity"[10].

So we return to a recurring problem, regardless of the strength of its economy or the military power generated by it, the communist regime that prevails in China constitutes, in itself, an obstacle to the organizational efficiency required the complexity of current weapon systems. It will be many years before this country can have the capacity of the United States to deploy and operate its armed forces in the place of the planet that requires it.

On the other hand, China has no military bases abroad; unlike the United States with bases in 76 countries. This installed capacity, together with that of its allies, facilitates the rapid and effective use of its military forces anywhere on the globe; whether for military campaigns such as those of the Persian Gulf wars, or in small operations focused on a small place on the planet, as in the case of actions against global terrorism.

Despite its hegemonic aspirations, China is only able to

make noise in much focused places of the planet, as it is the case of Sea of China. For its part, the United States allows that country to overtake from time to time and commits some outrage. As is the case of the construction of islands in the South China Sea or violations of the right to free navigation in these waters. Nothing that disrupts the established order and hinders the flow of goods in the China Sea. The United States looks the other way and China maintains its pride intact.

Notes

I

[1]The Economics, *Who is Chinese? The upper Han*, November 19 2016, digital edition.

II

[1]Carter, A., *The Rebalance and Asia-Pacific Security. Building a Principle Security Network*, Foreign Affairs, November-December 2016, pág. 66.
[2]Moscow's Failed Pivot to China, Foreign Affairs, April 17 2016, digital edition.
[3]Ibídem.
[4]Ibídem

III

[1]Hu Angang, *China's New Normal*, Foreign Affairs, *Embracing,* Mayo-Jun 2015, digital edition.
[2]The Economics, *Shadow Banks. Dark and Stormy*, London May 7 2016, digital edition.
[3]Ghemawat, P., y Hout, T., *Can China's Companies Conquer the World?,* Foreign Affairs, March-April 2016, págs. 86-98.
[4]The Economics, *China. A long march,* London, October 3 2015, digital edition.

IV

[1]Carter, A., *The Rebalance and Asia-Pacific Security. Building a Principle Security Network*, Foreign Affairs, November-December 2016, pág. 69.
[2] Lo. Cit.
[3]Loc. Cit.
[4]Ibídem, pág. 70
[5]Ibídem, págs. 69 y 70.
[6]Ibídem, pág. 70.

[7]Brooks, S., y Wohlforth, W., *The once and future superpower. Why China won´t overtake The United States*, Foreign Affairs, May-Jun 2016, pág. 96.

[8] Loc. Cit.

[9] Loc. Cit.

[10]Loc. Cit.